# Mastering Tableau: From Beginner to Advanced

A comprehensive guide that covers everything from the basics of Tableau to advanced visualization techniques, calculations, and data blending.

## Table of Contents

# Chapter 1: Introduction to Tableau

Welcome to "Mastering Tableau: From Beginner to Advanced." In this comprehensive guide, we will embark on a journey to explore the powerful world of Tableau, from its foundational concepts to advanced visualization techniques, calculations, and data blending. Whether you're a beginner taking your first steps in Tableau or an experienced user looking to expand your skills, this book aims to equip you with the knowledge and tools necessary to become a Tableau master.

## 1.1 What is Tableau?

Tableau is a leading data visualization and business intelligence software that enables users to connect to various data sources, create interactive visualizations, and gain insights from complex datasets. With Tableau's intuitive drag-and-drop interface and powerful analytical capabilities, users can easily transform data into visually appealing and interactive dashboards, reports, and charts.

## 1.2 The Importance of Tableau Skills

In today's data-driven world, the ability to effectively analyze and visualize data is crucial for decision-making, problem-solving, and identifying patterns and trends. Tableau empowers users to unlock the hidden stories within their data and communicate them effectively to a wide audience. By mastering Tableau, you will gain a competitive edge in the realm of data analytics and be able to extract meaningful insights from vast amounts of information.

## 1.3 What This Book Covers

This book is designed to be a comprehensive guide that covers the entire Tableau ecosystem, from the basics to advanced concepts. We will start by familiarizing ourselves with the Tableau interface, learning how to connect to various data sources, and exploring the different types of visualizations Tableau offers. As we progress, we will delve into more advanced topics such as calculations, parameters, and blending data from multiple sources.

The book covers

Introduction to Tableau

Getting Started with Tableau

In each chapter, we will provide clear explanations, step-by-step instructions, and practical examples to help you grasp the concepts and apply them in real-world scenarios. By the end of this book, you will have the skills and confidence to navigate Tableau proficiently and create compelling visualizations that drive impactful insights.

So, let's dive into the world of Tableau and embark on this exciting journey of mastering data visualization and analytics!

# Chapter 2: Getting Started with Tableau

## 2.1 Installing Tableau Desktop

To begin your Tableau journey, you'll first need to install Tableau Desktop on your computer. Follow these steps to get started:

Step 1: Visit the Tableau website at www.tableau.com and navigate to the "Products" section.

Step 2: Choose the appropriate version of Tableau Desktop for your operating system (Windows or Mac) and click on the download link.

Step 3: Once the download is complete, run the installer and follow the on-screen instructions to install Tableau Desktop.

Step 4: After the installation is complete, launch Tableau Desktop.

## 2.2 Exploring the Tableau Interface

When you launch Tableau Desktop, you'll be greeted with its user-friendly interface. Let's take a tour of the main components:

Menu Bar: Located at the top of the interface, the menu bar provides access to various commands and features in Tableau.

Toolbar: The toolbar contains frequently used tools such as the Save button, Undo/Redo buttons, and options for connecting to data sources.

Data Pane: On the left side of the interface, you'll find the Data pane. This is where you can view and manage the data sources, dimensions, and measures used in your visualizations.

Worksheets and Dashboards: In the center of the interface, you'll see the workspace area. This is where you'll create worksheets (individual visualizations) and dashboards (collections of multiple visualizations).

Show Me Panel: Located on the right side of the interface, the Show Me panel provides quick access to different types of visualizations that you can create in Tableau.

Marks Card and Shelves: Below the Show Me panel, you'll find the Marks card and shelves. These are used to define the visual encoding of your data, such as colors, size, and labels.

Data Source Tab: At the bottom of the interface, you'll see the Data Source tab. This tab allows you to view and edit the properties of your data source, including connections, joins, and calculations.

**2.3 Connecting to a Data Source**

Now that you're familiar with the Tableau interface, let's connect to a data source:

Step 1: Click on the "Connect to Data" button on the toolbar.

Step 2: Select the type of data source you want to connect to, such as Excel, CSV, a database, or a cloud service.

Step 3: Navigate to the location of your data source file and select it. If you're connecting to a database or cloud service, enter the required credentials.

Step 4: Tableau will automatically detect the structure of your data and display it in the Data pane. Review the data preview to ensure it's imported correctly.

**2.4 Creating Your First Visualization**

With your data source connected, let's create a basic visualization:

Step 1: Drag a dimension field from the Data pane (e.g., "Category") to the Columns shelf.

Step 2: Drag a measure field from the Data pane (e.g., "Sales") to the Rows shelf.

Step 3: Tableau will automatically generate a visualization based on your selections. You can customize the visualization further using the Marks card and shelves.

Step 4: To change the visualization type, explore the options in the Show Me panel and click on a different chart type.

Step 5: Format your visualization by adjusting colors, labels, and other properties using the formatting options available in the toolbar and the Marks card.

**2.5 Saving and Publishing Your Workbook**

Once you've created a visualization, it's important to save your work:

Step 1: Click on the "Save" button on the toolbar.

Step 2: Choose a location on your computer to save the Tableau workbook (.twb) file.

Step 3: To share your workbook with others, you can publish it to Tableau Server or Tableau Public. Click on the "Server" or "Public" options in the toolbar, and follow the instructions to publish your workbook.

Congratulations! You've successfully taken your first steps in Tableau. In this chapter, we covered the installation process, explored the Tableau interface, connected to a data source, created a basic visualization, and saved your workbook. In the following chapters, we'll dive deeper into Tableau's features and explore more advanced visualization techniques, calculations, and data blending.

# Chapter 3: Connecting to Data Sources

### 3.1 Exploring Data Connection Options

In Tableau, you have various options for connecting to different data sources. Let's explore some of the most common connection types:

Excel: To connect to an Excel file, click on the "Excel" option in the Connect pane. Navigate to the location of your Excel file and select it. Tableau will import the data into the Data pane.

CSV: If your data is in CSV format, select the "Text file" option in the Connect pane. Locate and choose the CSV file you want to connect to, and Tableau will import the data.

Databases: Tableau supports connections to a wide range of databases, including MySQL, PostgreSQL, Oracle, SQL Server, and more. Click on the "More" option in the Connect pane to explore the available database connection options.

Cloud Services: Tableau can connect to various cloud services, such as Google Analytics, Salesforce, Amazon

Redshift, and more. Choose the appropriate connector in the Connect pane and follow the prompts to connect to your cloud service.

Web Data Connectors: Tableau allows you to create or use custom Web Data Connectors to connect to web-based data sources that are not natively supported. Explore the "Web Data Connector" option in the Connect pane for more information.

### 3.2 Connecting to a Data Source

Now, let's connect to a specific data source using one of the connection options:

Step 1: Launch Tableau Desktop and click on the "Connect to Data" button on the toolbar.

Step 2: In the Connect pane, select the appropriate connection option based on your data source (e.g., Excel, CSV, database, etc.).

Step 3: Navigate to the location of your data source file or provide the necessary connection details, such as server name, database name, username, and password.

Step 4: Depending on the connection type, you may have additional options to configure, such as specifying the data range in an Excel file or writing a SQL query for a database connection. Adjust these settings as needed.

Step 5: Once you've configured the connection, click on the "Connect" button to establish the connection and import the data into Tableau.

### 3.3 Managing Data Source Connections

Tableau allows you to manage and modify your data source connections as needed. Here are some common tasks:

Editing Connections: To modify an existing connection, open the workbook that contains the connection, navigate to the Data Source tab, and click on the connection name. Tableau will prompt you to edit the connection details.

Adding Data to Existing Connections: You can add additional tables or files to an existing connection. In the Data Source tab, click on the "Add" button and follow the prompts to select the new data source and specify the join or relationship with the existing data.

Refreshing Data: To update the data in your Tableau workbook with the latest information from the data source, click on the "Refresh" button in the toolbar. Tableau will retrieve the updated data based on the connection settings.

Removing Connections: If you no longer need a connection, you can remove it from the workbook. In the Data Source tab, right-click on the connection name and select "Remove". Note that this action will remove all related worksheets and dashboards.

**3.4 Data Source Filters and Extracts**

Tableau provides options for applying filters and creating extracts from your data sources:

Data Source Filters: You can apply filters at the data source level to limit the data imported into Tableau. In the Data Source tab, select a table or data source, and click on the

"Add" button next to the Filters card. Define your filtering criteria and save the changes.

Data Extracts: To improve performance and work with large datasets, you can create data extracts. In the Data Source tab, click on the "Extract" button and follow the prompts to specify the data range and filtering options for the extract.

By effectively managing your data connections and leveraging Tableau's filtering and extract capabilities, you can ensure optimal performance and access the most relevant data for your analyses.

Congratulations! In this chapter, you learned about the various data connection options in Tableau, how to connect to different types of data sources, and how to manage and modify your data connections. In the next chapter, we'll delve deeper into exploring visualizations in Tableau and unleash its powerful analytical capabilities.

# Chapter 4: Exploring Visualizations in Tableau

## 4.1 Understanding the Visualization Types

Tableau offers a wide range of visualization types to help you present and analyze data effectively. Let's explore some of the most commonly used visualization types in Tableau:

Bar Chart: A bar chart represents data using horizontal or vertical bars, where the length or height of each bar corresponds to the data value.

Line Chart: A line chart shows data trends over time using connected data points, making it useful for visualizing data with continuous variables.

Pie Chart: A pie chart displays data as a circle divided into slices, where each slice represents a category and the size of the slice represents the proportion of data.

Scatter Plot: A scatter plot uses Cartesian coordinates to represent data points on a graph, making it ideal for exploring relationships between two numerical variables.

Map: Tableau offers robust mapping capabilities, allowing you to visualize data geographically by plotting it on a map, such as a world map or a custom region.

Tree Map: A tree map displays hierarchical data using nested rectangles, where the size of each rectangle represents the magnitude of a specific data attribute.

Heat Map: A heat map visualizes data using color gradients, allowing you to identify patterns or areas of concentration in a matrix or grid-like dataset.

Gantt Chart: A Gantt chart represents project timelines and tasks, displaying bars that indicate the duration and dependencies of each task.

These are just a few examples of the visualization types available in Tableau. Each type has its own purpose and is suitable for different data scenarios. As you become more proficient in Tableau, you can explore and experiment with additional visualization types to best represent your data.

## 4.2 Creating Basic Visualizations

Let's create some basic visualizations using different chart types in Tableau:

Step 1: Connect to a data source or open an existing workbook that contains data.

Step 2: Drag and drop a dimension field (e.g., "Category") onto the Columns shelf.

Step 3: Drag and drop a measure field (e.g., "Sales") onto the Rows shelf.

Step 4: Tableau will automatically generate a visualization based on the selected chart type (e.g., bar chart).

Step 5: To change the chart type, locate the Show Me panel on the right side of the interface. Click on a different chart type to instantly update the visualization.

Step 6: Experiment with additional dimensions or measures by dragging and dropping them onto the appropriate shelves.

Observe how the visualization dynamically updates to reflect the changes.

Step 7: Customize your visualization by adjusting properties in the Marks card and shelves. For example, you can change colors, labels, sorting, and axis formatting.

Step 8: To create more advanced visualizations, consider adding additional dimensions to the Color or Size shelves. This allows you to represent additional data attributes visually.

**4.3 Interacting with Visualizations**

Tableau provides interactivity features that allow users to explore and interact with visualizations:

Filter: You can filter the data displayed in a visualization by selecting a specific data point, category, or range of values. To apply a filter, click on a data point or use the Filter card in the top-right corner of the visualization.

Tooltip: Hovering over data points in a visualization displays tooltips that provide additional information about the data.

Drill Down and Drill Up: Tableau allows you to drill down into hierarchical data, exploring details at different levels, or drill up to view summarized data.

Parameter Control: Parameters enable users to dynamically change values, thresholds, or dimensions in a visualization, providing a more interactive experience.

By utilizing these interactive features, you can empower users to explore data in more depth and gain insights through interactive visual analysis.

**4.4 Formatting and Styling Visualizations**

Tableau provides extensive formatting options to enhance the visual appeal and clarity of your visualizations. Here are some formatting techniques:

Labels and Annotations: Add labels to data points or annotate specific areas of your visualization to provide additional context or highlight key insights.

Colors and Palettes: Customize the color scheme of your visualization to improve visual distinction, highlight specific data elements, or align with branding guidelines.

Axes and Gridlines: Adjust axis labels, scales, and gridlines to improve readability and better convey the magnitude or proportion of data.

Titles and Captions: Provide clear and descriptive titles and captions for your visualizations to help viewers understand the purpose and context of the data being presented.

Layout and Size: Arrange visualizations on a dashboard or worksheet to create a logical flow and optimize space utilization. Adjust the size of the visualization to fit the desired presentation medium.

Remember to strike a balance between aesthetics and effective communication when formatting your visualizations. Visual elements should enhance comprehension and not overshadow the data being presented.

Congratulations! In this chapter, you explored different visualization types in Tableau, created basic visualizations using various chart types, learned about interactivity features, and discovered formatting techniques to enhance your visualizations. In the next chapter, we'll delve into advanced chart types and customization options to unlock Tableau's full visual potential.

# Chapter 5: Advanced Chart Types and Customization

## 5.1 Exploring Advanced Chart Types

Tableau offers a wide array of advanced chart types that can help you convey complex relationships and patterns in your data. Let's explore some of these advanced chart types:

Dual-Axis Chart: A dual-axis chart combines two different chart types on the same axis, allowing you to visualize two measures with different scales or units.

Box Plot: A box plot displays the distribution of a dataset, including quartiles, outliers, and median values. It is useful for understanding the spread and skewness of data.

Waterfall Chart: A waterfall chart illustrates how an initial value changes incrementally, with positive and negative values, creating a visual representation of cumulative effect.

Pareto Chart: A Pareto chart combines a column chart with a line chart, representing both individual values and cumulative percentages. It helps prioritize and focus on significant factors contributing to an outcome.

Bullet Graph: A bullet graph displays a target, actual progress, and comparative measures in a single chart, providing a concise view of performance against goals or benchmarks.

Treemap: A treemap visualizes hierarchical data using nested rectangles. It allows you to compare sizes of different categories within the hierarchy.

Radial Chart: A radial chart, such as a radar or polar chart, displays data points along multiple axes originating from a central point. It is useful for comparing values across multiple dimensions.

These are just a few examples of advanced chart types available in Tableau. As you become more familiar with Tableau's capabilities, explore additional chart types to effectively convey specific insights and patterns in your data.

## 5.2 Customizing Visualizations

Tableau provides extensive customization options to tailor your visualizations to your specific requirements. Let's explore some of the key customization features:

Formatting Individual Data Points: Tableau allows you to customize the appearance of individual data points within a visualization. By right-clicking on a data point or selecting it, you can modify its color, shape, or size.

Conditional Formatting: Apply conditional formatting to your visualizations to highlight specific data points or ranges based on certain criteria. You can use color scales, data bars, or text formatting to emphasize important information.

Adding Reference Lines, Bands, and Boxes: Tableau enables you to include reference lines, bands, or boxes in your visualizations to provide context or mark important thresholds. These reference elements can be added from the Analytics pane or by right-clicking on the visualization.

Calculated Fields and Expressions: Use calculated fields and expressions to create custom calculations that go beyond the available dimensions and measures. By combining existing fields or applying mathematical functions, you can create new insights.

Interactive Filters and Parameters: Leverage the power of interactive filters and parameters to enable users to dynamically change values, dimensions, or thresholds within a visualization. This enhances the interactive experience and allows for on-the-fly analysis.

Tooltips and Annotations: Customize tooltips to display additional information or include rich text formatting. Add annotations to highlight specific data points or provide context within the visualization.

By utilizing these customization options, you can create visually engaging and tailored visualizations that effectively communicate insights from your data.

**5.3 Dashboard Design Best Practices**

Dashboards in Tableau allow you to combine multiple visualizations into a single view. Here are some best practices for designing effective dashboards:

Focus on Key Insights: Identify the key insights or messages you want to convey through your dashboard. Keep the layout clean and avoid clutter to ensure the most important information stands out.

Use Appropriate Visualizations: Select visualizations that best represent the data and insights. Consider the data type, relationships, and the story you want to tell.

Maintain Consistency: Use a consistent color scheme, font styles, and formatting across your visualizations to create a cohesive and professional look. Consistency helps users navigate the dashboard easily.

Utilize Layout Containers: Use layout containers, such as horizontal or vertical layouts, to organize and group related visualizations. This improves the overall structure and readability of the dashboard.

Interactive Elements: Incorporate interactive elements like filters, parameters, or actions within the dashboard to enable users to explore the data further. This encourages engagement and deeper analysis.

Test and Iterate: Continuously test your dashboard design with different user perspectives and iterate based on feedback. Regularly review and update your dashboards as data or requirements change.

Remember, the goal of a dashboard is to provide a clear and concise overview of your data and insights. Design with the end user in mind, ensuring that the dashboard facilitates their understanding and decision-making processes.

Congratulations! In this chapter, you explored advanced chart types and customization options in Tableau. You learned about advanced visualization types like dual-axis charts, box plots, and bullet graphs. You also discovered how to customize visualizations, including formatting individual data points, applying conditional formatting, and adding reference lines. Lastly, you explored best practices for designing effective dashboards. In the next chapter, we will delve into calculations and expressions in Tableau, unlocking the power to derive deeper insights from your data.

# Chapter 6: Working with Calculations and Expressions

## 6.1 Introduction to Calculations and Expressions

Calculations and expressions in Tableau allow you to perform complex calculations, manipulate data, and derive meaningful insights. Let's explore the basics of working with calculations and expressions:

Calculated Fields: Calculated fields are user-defined formulas that create new fields based on existing fields in your data. They can be used to perform mathematical operations, concatenate strings, apply logical conditions, and more.

Aggregations: Aggregations are functions used to summarize data, such as calculating sums, averages, counts, or minimum/maximum values. Aggregations can be applied within calculated fields to generate meaningful metrics.

Table Calculations: Table calculations are calculations performed on the result set of your visualization. They can be used to calculate running totals, percent of total, moving averages, and other window calculations.

Level of Detail (LOD) Expressions: LOD expressions allow you to perform calculations at different levels of detail than what is specified in your visualization. They provide control over the granularity of your analysis and help answer specific questions about subsets of your data.

## 6.2 Creating Calculated Fields

Let's create a simple calculated field in Tableau:

Step 1: In your Tableau worksheet, navigate to the Analysis menu and select "Create Calculated Field".

Step 2: In the calculation editor that appears, provide a name for your calculated field.

Step 3: Write the calculation using Tableau's formula syntax. For example, you can calculate the profit margin by subtracting the cost from the sales and dividing it by sales: (SUM([Sales]) - SUM([Cost])) / SUM([Sales]).

Step 4: Click "OK" to save the calculated field.

## 6.3 Using Aggregations and Functions

Tableau provides a wide range of built-in functions and aggregations that can be used within calculated fields. Let's explore some common ones:

SUM(): Calculates the sum of a specified field or expression.

AVG(): Calculates the average of a specified field or expression.

COUNT(): Counts the number of non-null values in a specified field or expression.

MIN(): Returns the minimum value from a specified field or expression.

MAX(): Returns the maximum value from a specified field or expression.

IF-ELSE Statements: Tableau allows you to write conditional statements within calculated fields using IF-ELSE logic. For example, you can create a calculated field to categorize sales as "High" if they exceed a certain threshold, and "Low" otherwise.

**6.4 Table Calculations**

Table calculations are powerful tools for performing calculations based on the structure of your visualization. Let's create a simple table calculation:

Step 1: In your Tableau worksheet, right-click on a measure in your view and select "Add Table Calculation".

Step 2: Choose the type of table calculation you want to perform, such as running total, percent of total, or moving average.

Step 3: Configure the table calculation by specifying the partitioning, addressing, and sorting options based on your analysis needs.

Step 4: Click "OK" to apply the table calculation to your visualization.

### 6.5 Level of Detail (LOD) Expressions

LOD expressions enable you to perform calculations at different levels of detail than what is displayed in your visualization. Let's create a simple LOD expression:

Step 1: In your Tableau worksheet, navigate to the Analysis menu and select "Create Calculated Field".

Step 2: In the calculation editor, write the LOD expression using Tableau's LOD syntax. For example, you can calculate the average sales per customer across all products using the following expression: { FIXED [Customer ID] : AVG([Sales]) }.

Step 3: Click "OK" to save the LOD expression.

### 6.6 Using Parameters in Calculations

Parameters in Tableau allow you to create dynamic inputs that users can adjust. You can incorporate parameters within your calculations to provide more interactivity. Let's use a parameter in a calculation:

Step 1: Create a parameter by right-clicking in the Data pane and selecting "Create Parameter". Define the parameter properties, such as data type, range, or list of values.

Step 2: In your calculated field, use the parameter by referencing its name within the calculation. For example, you can create a calculated field to filter data based on a parameter-defined threshold.

Step 3: Adjust the parameter value in your worksheet to see the impact on the calculated field and the visualization.

By utilizing calculated fields, aggregations, table calculations, LOD expressions, and parameters, you can perform complex calculations and derive deeper insights from your data in Tableau.

Congratulations! In this chapter, you explored the basics of working with calculations and expressions in Tableau. You learned how to create calculated fields, use aggregations and functions, perform table calculations, leverage LOD expressions, and incorporate parameters within calculations.

In the next chapter, we will dive into parameters and filters in Tableau, enabling you to further refine your visualizations and analysis.

# Chapter 7: Parameters and Filters in Tableau

## 7.1 Introduction to Parameters

Parameters in Tableau allow you to create dynamic inputs that users can adjust, providing interactivity and flexibility in your visualizations. Let's explore the basics of working with parameters:

Creating Parameters: To create a parameter, right-click in the Data pane and select "Create Parameter". Define the parameter properties such as name, data type, range, or list of values.

Parameter Types: Tableau offers different types of parameters, including continuous (allowing users to adjust a range of values) and discrete (providing a list of predefined values).

Using Parameters in Calculations: Parameters can be incorporated within calculations to make them dynamic. By referencing a parameter within a calculated field, you enable users to adjust its value and see the impact on the visualization.

## 7.2 Applying Filters to Visualizations

Filters allow you to limit the data displayed in your visualizations, providing focused insights. Let's explore how to apply filters in Tableau:

Step 1: In your Tableau worksheet, locate the Dimensions or Measures pane.

Step 2: Drag a field onto the Filters shelf or right-click on a field and select "Add to Filters".

Step 3: Adjust the filter options based on your analysis needs. You can filter by specific values, ranges, or conditions.

Step 4: Apply the filter to your visualization by clicking the "Apply" or "OK" button in the filter dialog.

**7.3 Using Parameters as Filters**

Parameters can also be used as filters to allow users to dynamically adjust the data displayed in a visualization. Let's use a parameter as a filter:

Step 1: Create a parameter by right-clicking in the Data pane and selecting "Create Parameter". Define the parameter properties, such as name, data type, range, or list of values.

Step 2: Drag the desired field onto the Filters shelf.

Step 3: In the filter dialog, select the "Use All" option, then click on the drop-down arrow beside the field name.

Step 4: Choose "By Formula" from the drop-down list and write a formula that incorporates the parameter. For example, you can filter by values greater than the parameter value.

Step 5: Click "OK" to apply the filter.

## 7.4 Creating Interactive Dashboards with Parameters and Filters

Parameters and filters can be combined to create interactive dashboards that allow users to explore data dynamically. Let's create an interactive dashboard:

Step 1: Create parameters and filters based on the fields and dimensions you want to provide interactivity for.

Step 2: Design your dashboard by dragging visualizations onto the canvas.

Step 3: Apply filters to each visualization by clicking on the drop-down arrow in the top-right corner of the visualization and selecting "Apply to Worksheets > Selected Worksheets".

Step 4: Add parameter controls to your dashboard by dragging them from the Objects pane onto the canvas.

Step 5: Link the parameter controls to the appropriate visualizations by right-clicking on a parameter control, selecting "Apply to Worksheets > Selected Worksheets", and choosing the target visualizations.

Step 6: Test your interactive dashboard by adjusting the parameter controls and observing how the visualizations and filters respond.

## 7.5 Dynamic Set Creation with Parameters

Parameters can also be used to dynamically create sets based on user-defined criteria. Let's create a dynamic set using a parameter:

Step 1: Create a parameter that represents the condition or criteria for the set.

Step 2: Create a calculated field that evaluates the parameter condition and returns a Boolean result. For example, you can create a calculated field that checks if a sales value is above the parameter-defined threshold.

Step 3: Use the calculated field to create a dynamic set by right-clicking on the field and selecting "Create > Set". Choose the "Use All" option in the set dialog and define the condition using the parameter.

Step 4: Apply the dynamic set to your visualization by dragging it onto the Filters shelf or using it as a dimension.

**7.6 Customizing Parameter Controls**

Tableau provides options for customizing the appearance and behavior of parameter controls. Let's explore some customization features:

Formatting: Format parameter controls to match the style and theme of your dashboard by adjusting font size, color, alignment, and other formatting options.

Display Options: Choose how the parameter control is displayed, such as a drop-down list, slider, or type-in box, based on the type and range of values.

Default Values: Set default values for parameters to provide initial settings for users when they interact with the dashboard.

Allowable Values: Control the allowable values for parameters by defining a range, list, or calculation that restricts the user's input.

By utilizing parameters and filters, you can create interactive dashboards, enable dynamic filtering, and empower users to explore data with flexibility.

Congratulations! In this chapter, you learned about parameters and filters in Tableau. You explored the creation and use of parameters, applying filters to visualizations, using parameters as filters, and creating interactive dashboards with parameters and filters. Additionally, you discovered how to create dynamic sets using parameters and customize parameter controls. In the next chapter, we will explore data blending and joining in Tableau, enabling you to combine data from multiple sources for more comprehensive analysis.

# Chapter 8: Data Blending and Joins in Tableau

## 8.1 Introduction to Data Blending and Joins

Data blending and joins in Tableau allow you to combine data from multiple sources to perform comprehensive analysis. Let's explore the basics of data blending and joins:

Data Blending: Data blending is the process of combining data from different sources that have a common field or relationship. It allows you to work with data from separate databases, Excel files, or other sources in a single Tableau workbook.

Joins: Joins are used to combine related data from different tables within the same data source. They allow you to merge data based on a common field or key, such as a customer ID or product code.

## 8.2 Data Blending in Tableau

Let's explore how to perform data blending in Tableau:

Step 1: Connect to your first data source as you normally would by clicking on the "Connect to Data" button.

Step 2: Drag and drop the required dimensions and measures onto the worksheet to create a visualization.

Step 3: Connect to the second data source by clicking on the "Connect to Data" button again. Tableau will detect the existing data source and prompt you to blend the data.

Step 4: Select the common field or relationship between the two data sources to blend the data. Tableau will automatically create a relationship based on this field.

Step 5: Drag and drop dimensions and measures from the second data source onto the worksheet to incorporate them into your visualization.

### 8.3 Joining Tables in Tableau

To join tables within the same data source, follow these steps:

Step 1: Connect to your data source by clicking on the "Connect to Data" button.

Step 2: Drag the required tables onto the canvas.

Step 3: Identify the common field or key that exists in both tables. This field will be used to join the tables.

Step 4: Click and drag the common field from one table to the matching field in the other table. Tableau will create the join based on the field relationship.

Step 5: Choose the appropriate join type, such as inner join, left join, right join, or full outer join, based on your data requirements.

Step 6: Once the tables are joined, you can use dimensions and measures from both tables in your visualizations.

**8.4 Managing Data Relationships and Join Types**

Tableau provides options to manage data relationships and choose the appropriate join types. Let's explore these features:

Edit Relationships: To modify the relationship between blended data sources or tables, navigate to the Data Source tab. Right-click on the connection and select "Edit Relationship". Adjust the join fields, join type, or other settings as needed.

Adding Additional Tables: You can add more tables to an existing data source or blend additional data sources by clicking on the "Add" button in the Data Source tab. Follow the prompts to specify the relationship and join type.

Join Types: When joining tables, you have different options for join types based on your data requirements:

Inner Join: Returns only the records with matching values in both tables.

Left Join: Returns all records from the left table and the matching records from the right table.

Right Join: Returns all records from the right table and the matching records from the left table.

Full Outer Join: Returns all records from both tables, including unmatched records.

Choose the appropriate join type based on the relationship between your data and the desired result.

**8.5 Blending and Joining Data with Different Granularities**

When blending or joining data, you may encounter scenarios where the data sources or tables have different levels of granularity. Tableau provides options to handle these situations:

Aggregation: If you have data at different levels of granularity, Tableau automatically aggregates the data based on the level of detail in your visualization. You can control the aggregation by adjusting the dimensions and measures used in your visualizations.

Data Densification: Tableau's data densification feature allows you to generate additional data points to match the granularity of the visualizations. This ensures that data from different sources align correctly.

Data Preprocessing: In some cases, you may need to preprocess or reshape your data to ensure consistent granularity before blending or joining. This can be done using Tableau's data preparation features or by using data transformation tools outside of Tableau.

**8.6 Data Source Filters and Extracts in Blended Data**

When working with blended data, you can apply data source filters and create extracts to optimize performance:

Data Source Filters: Tableau allows you to apply filters to individual data sources in a blended environment. Right-click on a data source in the Data pane and select "Add to Context" to create a filter specific to that data source.

Extracts: To improve performance in blended data scenarios, you can create data extracts. Extracts allow you to extract and store a subset of data from each data source, which can significantly enhance query and rendering speeds.

By mastering the art of data blending and joining in Tableau, you can leverage multiple data sources to perform comprehensive analysis and gain deeper insights.

Congratulations! In this chapter, you learned about data blending and joins in Tableau. You explored the process of blending data from different sources, joining tables within the same data source, and managing data relationships and join types. Additionally, you discovered how to handle blended data with different granularities and apply data source filters and extracts. In the next chapter, we will delve into geographic and spatial analysis in Tableau, enabling you to visualize and analyze data based on geographic information.

# Chapter 9: Geographic and Spatial Analysis in Tableau

## 9.1 Introduction to Geographic and Spatial Analysis

Tableau provides powerful tools for geographic and spatial analysis, allowing you to visualize and analyze data based on geographic information. Let's explore the basics of working with geographic and spatial data in Tableau:

Geographic Roles: Tableau automatically recognizes geographic fields, such as country, state, city, or latitude/longitude, and assigns them geographic roles. These roles enable Tableau to generate map visualizations and perform spatial analysis.

Map Layers: Tableau offers various map layers, including background maps, data layers, and reference layers. Background maps provide the visual context, data layers represent your data geographically, and reference layers provide additional context, such as boundaries or landmarks.

Geographic Operations: Tableau allows you to perform spatial operations, such as distance calculations, spatial joins, and geographic aggregations. These operations help uncover insights and patterns in your geographic data.

**9.2 Creating Map Visualizations**

Let's explore how to create map visualizations in Tableau:

Step 1: Connect to a data source that contains geographic fields, such as latitude and longitude, or fields recognized as geographic roles.

Step 2: Drag a geographic field, such as Country or State, onto the Rows or Columns shelf.

Step 3: Tableau will automatically generate a map visualization based on the geographic field. You can further customize the map by adding additional dimensions or measures to the Marks card or adjusting the map options in the Map Layers pane.

Step 4: Use the map toolbar to zoom, pan, or interact with the map. You can also apply filters or highlight specific data points using the map's functionality.

### 9.3 Working with Background Maps and Map Layers

Tableau provides various background maps and map layers to enhance your geographic visualizations. Let's explore these options:

Background Maps: Tableau offers a variety of background map styles, including basic maps, satellite imagery, and custom map styles. You can select the desired background map by clicking on the Map Layers pane and choosing a map style from the Background Maps section.

Data Layers: Data layers allow you to plot your data geographically. You can drag dimensions or measures onto the Marks card to represent your data using different map elements, such as points, lines, or polygons.

Reference Layers: Reference layers provide additional context to your map visualizations. You can add reference layers, such as country borders, state boundaries, or landmarks, by clicking on the Map Layers pane and selecting the desired reference layer from the available options.

**9.4 Geographic Operations and Analysis**

Tableau enables you to perform spatial operations and analysis on your geographic data. Let's explore some of these capabilities:

Distance Calculations: Tableau allows you to calculate distances between geographic points using spatial calculations. You can measure distances between cities, find the nearest locations, or calculate driving distances.

Spatial Joins: You can perform spatial joins to combine data based on geographic relationships. For example, you can join demographic data with geographic boundaries to analyze population density or combine sales data with store locations to study regional performance.

Geographic Aggregations: Tableau provides geographic aggregations that summarize data within specific geographic boundaries. You can aggregate data by country, state, or any custom boundaries to examine regional patterns or compare performance across regions.

## 9.5 Geocoding and Mapping Custom Locations

Tableau allows you to geocode and map custom locations that may not be recognized as geographic fields. Let's explore how to work with custom locations:

Step 1: Ensure that your data contains a field with the names or addresses of the custom locations.

Step 2: Right-click on the field containing the custom locations and select "Geocode". Tableau will attempt to match the locations with latitude and longitude coordinates.

Step 3: If Tableau is unable to geocode the locations automatically, you can use a geocoding service or a separate data source that provides the latitude and longitude information for the custom locations. You can then join this data source with your primary data source using a common field.

Step 4: Once the custom locations are geocoded, you can plot them on a map visualization and perform geographic analysis similar to standard geographic fields.

## 9.6 Using Spatial Filters and Calculations

Tableau provides spatial filters and calculations to further refine your geographic analysis. Let's explore these features:

Spatial Filters: You can apply spatial filters to focus on specific areas or regions within your map visualization. For example, you can filter by a particular country or region to isolate and analyze data at a more granular level.

Spatial Calculations: Tableau offers spatial calculations that allow you to create custom calculations based on geographic information. For example, you can calculate the area of polygons, create buffers around points of interest, or determine the intersections of geographic features.

By harnessing the power of geographic and spatial analysis in Tableau, you can visualize and analyze data in the context of location, uncovering valuable insights and patterns.

Congratulations! In this chapter, you learned about geographic and spatial analysis in Tableau. You explored how to create map visualizations, work with background maps and map layers, perform geographic operations and analysis, geocode and map custom locations, and utilize spatial filters and calculations. In the next chapter, we will delve into advanced analytics in Tableau, unlocking capabilities for statistical analysis, forecasting, and more.

# Chapter 10: Advanced Analytics in Tableau

## 10.1 Introduction to Advanced Analytics in Tableau

Tableau provides advanced analytics capabilities that allow you to perform statistical analysis, forecasting, and other advanced calculations. Let's explore the basics of working with advanced analytics in Tableau:

Statistical Analysis: Tableau offers a range of statistical functions and calculations that enable you to analyze data distributions, correlations, trends, and more.

Forecasting: Tableau allows you to perform time series forecasting to predict future values based on historical data. This is particularly useful for analyzing trends and making data-driven projections.

Clustering: Tableau supports clustering algorithms that group similar data points together based on their attributes. Clustering helps identify patterns and segments within your data.

Regression Analysis: Tableau provides regression models that allow you to analyze the relationship between variables and make predictions based on their interdependencies.

**10.2 Performing Statistical Analysis**

Let's explore how to perform statistical analysis in Tableau:

Step 1: Connect to a data source that contains the data you want to analyze statistically.

Step 2: Drag the desired variables onto the worksheet.

Step 3: To access statistical functions and calculations, navigate to the Analysis menu and select "Create Calculated Field" or "Add Table Calculation".

Step 4: Choose the appropriate statistical function or calculation based on your analysis needs. Tableau offers functions like SUM, AVG, COUNT, MIN, MAX, CORR, STDDEV, and more.

Step 5: Apply the statistical calculations to your visualization and explore the insights revealed by the analysis.

**10.3 Time Series Forecasting**

Let's explore how to perform time series forecasting in Tableau:

Step 1: Connect to a data source that contains historical time series data.

Step 2: Create a line chart or other appropriate visualization to display the historical data.

Step 3: Right-click on the visualization and select "Forecast" from the context menu.

Step 4: Adjust the forecast options, such as the forecast length, confidence interval, and seasonality settings.

Step 5: Tableau will generate a forecast line or band, indicating the predicted values and the range of uncertainty for future time periods.

Step 6: Analyze the forecasted values and use them to make data-driven projections or identify potential trends and patterns.

## 10.4 Utilizing Clustering

Let's explore how to utilize clustering in Tableau:

Step 1: Connect to a data source that contains the variables you want to cluster.

Step 2: Drag the variables onto the worksheet.

Step 3: Navigate to the Analysis menu and select "Create Clusters" or "Cluster" based on the version of Tableau you are using.

Step 4: Adjust the clustering options, such as the number of clusters or the distance metric to be used.

Step 5: Tableau will assign data points to different clusters based on their similarities and display the results on the visualization.

Step 6: Analyze the clusters and identify patterns or segments within your data based on their characteristics.

## 10.5 Performing Regression Analysis

Let's explore how to perform regression analysis in Tableau:

Step 1: Connect to a data source that contains the variables you want to analyze using regression.

Step 2: Drag the dependent variable and independent variables onto the worksheet.

Step 3: Navigate to the Analysis menu and select "Regression" or "Trend Line" based on the version of Tableau you are using.

Step 4: Tableau will generate a regression line or curve that represents the relationship between the dependent and independent variables.

Step 5: Analyze the regression results, including the coefficients, p-values, and goodness-of-fit measures, to understand the strength and significance of the relationship.

Step 6: Use the regression model to make predictions or forecast future values based on the independent variables.

**10.6 Incorporating Advanced Analytics into Dashboards**

Tableau allows you to incorporate advanced analytics into dashboards to provide interactive and dynamic insights. Let's explore how to do this:

Step 1: Design your dashboard by adding appropriate visualizations and controls.

Step 2: Integrate advanced analytics results, such as statistical analysis, forecasts, clustering, or regression models, into the dashboard by adding calculated fields, reference lines, or trend lines.

Step 3: Use parameter controls or filters to allow users to interact with the analytics results and explore different scenarios.

Step 4: Test the dashboard and ensure that the advanced analytics elements provide valuable insights and enhance the overall data-driven narrative.

By leveraging advanced analytics capabilities in Tableau, you can gain deeper insights, make data-driven predictions, and uncover patterns and trends within your data.

Congratulations! In this chapter, you learned about advanced analytics in Tableau. You explored how to perform statistical analysis, time series forecasting, clustering, and regression analysis. Additionally, you discovered how to incorporate advanced analytics into dashboards to provide interactive insights. In the next chapter, we will explore storytelling and data presentation techniques in Tableau, enabling you to effectively communicate your data findings and engage your audience.

# Chapter 11: Storytelling and Data Presentation in Tableau

## 11.1 Introduction to Storytelling and Data Presentation in Tableau

Tableau provides powerful tools for storytelling and data presentation, allowing you to create compelling narratives and communicate your data findings effectively. Let's explore the basics of storytelling and data presentation in Tableau:

Story Points: Tableau's Story Points feature enables you to create interactive presentations by combining visualizations, text, and annotations into a cohesive story.

Story Flow: A well-crafted data story has a clear flow that guides the audience through the narrative. It should have a logical structure, starting with an introduction, building up to key insights, and concluding with a call to action or summary.

Visual Design: Visual design plays a crucial role in data presentation. Tableau offers various design elements and formatting options that allow you to enhance the aesthetics and readability of your visualizations.

## 11.2 Creating a Data Story with Story Points

Let's explore how to create a data story using Story Points in Tableau:

Step 1: Open a new worksheet or dashboard in Tableau.

Step 2: Drag the visualizations you want to include in your story onto the canvas. Arrange and format them to convey your message effectively.

Step 3: Click on the "New Story" tab at the bottom of the Tableau window to enter Story Points mode.

Step 4: In the Story Points pane, click on the "+" button to add a new story point. Each story point represents a slide or page in your data story.

Step 5: Customize each story point by adding visualizations, text, annotations, and other elements. You can also adjust the layout and formatting to create a visually appealing narrative.

Step 6: Use the navigation controls in the Story Points pane to preview and refine your data story.

## 11.3 Crafting a Compelling Story Flow

To create a compelling story flow in Tableau, follow these guidelines:

Introduction: Start your data story with a captivating introduction that provides context and captures the audience's attention. Clearly state the purpose and objective of your analysis.

Building the Narrative: Progressively build your story by presenting the main findings and insights in a logical sequence. Use visualizations, annotations, and text to explain the key points and support your analysis.

Structured Transitions: Ensure smooth transitions between story points by adding connecting text or visuals that guide the audience from one insight to the next. This helps maintain the flow and coherence of your narrative.

Highlighting Key Findings: Emphasize the most important insights by using larger visualizations, bold text, or color enhancements. Draw the audience's attention to the key takeaways of your analysis.

Providing Context: Include relevant background information or contextual details that help the audience understand the data and its implications. This could include explanations of data sources, methodologies, or industry trends.

Conclusion and Call to Action: Conclude your data story with a summary of the key findings and insights. Consider including a call to action, such as recommendations, next steps, or opportunities for further exploration.

## 11.4 Enhancing Visual Design for Impactful Presentations

To enhance the visual design of your data presentation in Tableau, consider the following tips:

Color and Contrast: Choose a color palette that is visually pleasing and effectively conveys your message. Ensure that there is sufficient contrast between data elements and background to enhance readability.

Typography: Use appropriate font styles and sizes to ensure legibility. Consider using headings, subheadings, and body text to organize information and create hierarchy.

Layout and Composition: Arrange visualizations and text in a balanced and visually appealing manner. Pay attention to alignment, spacing, and symmetry to create a cohesive and professional look.

Annotation and Callouts: Use annotations or callouts to provide additional context or highlight specific data points. These elements can draw attention to important insights and enhance the storytelling experience.

Animation and Interactivity: Leverage Tableau's animation and interactivity features to engage your audience. Use transitions, tooltips, or filters to make your data story interactive and allow users to explore the visualizations further.

**11.5 Presenting and Sharing Your Data Story**

To present and share your data story created in Tableau, consider the following options:

Full-Screen Mode: Enter full-screen mode in Tableau to present your data story without any distractions. This mode provides a focused view of your visualizations and allows you to navigate through story points seamlessly.

Export as PDF or Image: Tableau allows you to export your data story as a PDF or image file. This is useful for sharing the presentation with others or incorporating it into other documents or slide decks.

Publish to Tableau Server or Tableau Public: If you have access to Tableau Server or Tableau Public, you can publish your data story online and share it as a web-based interactive presentation. This enables others to view and interact with your visualizations.

Embed in Websites or Blogs: Tableau provides embed options that allow you to integrate your data story into websites, blogs, or other online platforms. This enables you to reach a wider audience and engage with readers on external platforms.

**11.6 Iterating and Refining Your Data Story**

To ensure the effectiveness of your data story, it's important to iterate and refine it based on feedback and observations. Consider the following steps:

Seek Feedback: Share your data story with colleagues, stakeholders, or other experts in the field to gather feedback and insights. Listen to their perspectives and incorporate constructive suggestions.

Test and Revise: Present your data story to a test audience and observe their reactions and understanding. Make note of any areas that may require clarification or improvement, and iterate accordingly.

Update and Adapt: Keep your data story up to date as new data becomes available or as the analysis evolves. Update visualizations, insights, and conclusions to ensure relevance and accuracy.

By mastering the art of storytelling and data presentation in Tableau, you can effectively communicate your data findings and engage your audience in a compelling and impactful way.

Congratulations! In this chapter, you learned about storytelling and data presentation in Tableau. You explored how to create a data story using Story Points, craft a compelling story flow, enhance visual design, and present and share your data story. Additionally, you discovered the importance of iterating and refining

# Chapter 12: Dashboard Design Best Practices in Tableau

## 12.1 Introduction to Dashboard Design in Tableau

Designing effective and visually appealing dashboards is essential for presenting data in Tableau. In this chapter, we will explore best practices and techniques to create impactful and user-friendly dashboards. Let's dive into dashboard design in Tableau:

Purpose and Audience: Understand the purpose of your dashboard and the intended audience. This will guide your design decisions and help you create a dashboard that delivers the right insights to the right people.

Simplicity and Clarity: Keep your dashboard design simple and focused. Strive for clarity by using clear headings, concise labels, and intuitive visualizations. Avoid clutter and unnecessary elements that can distract from the main message.

Layout and Composition: Plan the layout of your dashboard carefully. Organize elements in a logical manner, considering the flow of information and the hierarchy of importance.

Balance the use of white space to create a visually pleasing composition.

**12.2 Choosing the Right Visualizations**

Selecting appropriate visualizations is crucial for conveying information effectively. Consider the following factors when choosing visualizations for your Tableau dashboard:

Data Types: Understand the type of data you are working with, such as categorical, numerical, time series, or geographic. Choose visualizations that best represent and highlight the characteristics of your data.

Message and Insights: Identify the key insights and messages you want to communicate through your dashboard. Select visualizations that effectively convey those insights and support the narrative.

User Experience: Consider the user's perspective and the level of interactivity required. Choose visualizations that allow users to explore the data and interact with the dashboard intuitively.

## 12.3 Designing Clear and Intuitive Navigation

Navigation is an important aspect of dashboard design. Here are some tips for creating clear and intuitive navigation in Tableau:

Dashboard Containers: Use containers to group related visualizations and elements. Organize them in a logical order, making it easy for users to navigate and understand the dashboard structure.

Dashboard Actions: Utilize dashboard actions to create interactivity and allow users to drill down or filter data based on their selections. Clearly communicate how users can interact with the dashboard and provide feedback through tooltips or instructional text.

Navigation Buttons: Incorporate navigation buttons or tabs to allow users to switch between different views or sections of the dashboard. Clearly label the buttons and provide visual cues to indicate the active view.

## 12.4 Effective Use of Color and Formatting

Color and formatting play a crucial role in dashboard design. Consider the following tips for effective use of color and formatting in Tableau:

Color Palette: Choose a color palette that aligns with your data and the message you want to convey. Use colors strategically to highlight important information and create visual hierarchy. Avoid excessive use of bright or clashing colors that can be overwhelming.

Consistent Formatting: Maintain consistency in formatting across the dashboard. Use consistent font styles, sizes, and colors for headings, labels, and text. This creates a cohesive and professional look.

Attention to Detail: Pay attention to details such as gridlines, axes, and labels. Ensure they are properly aligned, labeled, and formatted for clarity. Adjust the font size and axis scales to provide a comfortable reading experience.

**12.5 Responsiveness and Device Compatibility**

Creating responsive dashboards that are compatible with different devices is essential. Follow these tips for ensuring responsiveness and device compatibility in Tableau:

Device Preview: Use Tableau's device preview feature to test how your dashboard looks on different devices and screen sizes. Adjust the layout and sizing as needed to ensure a seamless experience across devices.

Grid Layout: Utilize Tableau's grid layout feature to create a flexible and responsive dashboard. Align elements to the grid and set appropriate column and row sizes that adapt well to different screen sizes.

Dashboard Size: Set the appropriate size for your dashboard based on the intended display device. Consider the aspect ratio and screen resolution to optimize the viewing experience.

## 12.6 Iteration and User Feedback

Iterate and gather feedback on your dashboard design to refine and improve its effectiveness. Consider the following steps:

Prototype and Test: Create a prototype of your dashboard and test it with representative users or stakeholders. Observe their interactions and gather feedback on usability, clarity, and visual appeal.

Incorporate Feedback: Analyze the feedback received and make necessary adjustments to the design. Consider suggestions for improving the layout, visualizations, navigation, or interactivity.

Continuous Improvement: Continue to iterate and refine your dashboard based on ongoing user feedback and evolving data needs. Regularly update the dashboard to reflect changes in the data or user requirements.

By following these best practices for dashboard design in Tableau, you can create visually appealing, user-friendly, and impactful dashboards that effectively communicate your data insights.

Congratulations! In this chapter, you learned about dashboard design best practices in Tableau. You explored the importance of purpose and audience, simplicity and clarity, layout and composition, choosing the rightvisualizations, designing clear and intuitive navigation, effective use of color and formatting, responsiveness and device compatibility, and iteration based on user feedback. By implementing these best practices, you can create dashboards that effectively communicate data insights and engage your audience. In the next chapter, we will explore advanced techniques and tips for optimizing performance and scalability in Tableau.

# Chapter 13: Performance Optimization and Scalability in Tableau

## 13.1 Introduction to Performance Optimization and Scalability

Optimizing performance and ensuring scalability are crucial when working with large datasets and complex visualizations in Tableau. In this chapter, we will explore advanced techniques and tips to enhance the performance and scalability of your Tableau workbooks. Let's dive into performance optimization and scalability in Tableau:

Data Source Optimization: Optimize your data sources to ensure efficient querying and processing of data.

Calculation Efficiency: Improve the efficiency of calculations and data blending operations to reduce processing time.

Visualization Design: Design visualizations that are optimized for performance and scalability.

Tableau Server Configuration: Configure Tableau Server settings to maximize performance and handle increasing user loads.

## 13.2 Data Source Optimization

To optimize your data sources in Tableau, consider the following techniques:

Data Extraction: Extract subsets of data and create Tableau data extracts (.tde or .hyper files). Extracts can improve query performance, especially when working with large datasets or remote data sources.

Filtering and Aggregation: Apply filters and aggregations at the data source level to reduce the amount of data transferred and processed in Tableau. Use data source filters, calculated fields, or aggregated extracts to optimize performance.

Custom SQL: Utilize custom SQL queries to optimize data retrieval from your database. Write efficient queries that fetch only the required data, apply appropriate filters, and leverage database-specific optimizations.

Incremental Refreshes: If your data source is frequently updated, consider implementing incremental refreshes. This ensures that only the updated data is refreshed, reducing the overall processing time.

## 13.3 Calculation Efficiency

To improve the efficiency of calculations and data blending operations, consider the following techniques:

Minimize Calculated Fields: Limit the number of calculated fields in your workbook. Excessive calculated fields can slow down workbook performance, especially when dealing with complex calculations.

Simplify Calculations: Simplify complex calculations by breaking them down into smaller, more manageable calculations. Avoid redundant or unnecessary calculations and ensure they are optimized for performance.

Use Tableau Functions: Leverage Tableau's built-in functions and features, such as table calculations, LOD (Level of Detail) expressions, and data blending optimizations. These functions are designed for efficiency and can help improve performance.

Evaluate Aggregation Options: Choose the appropriate aggregation options, such as aggregating data at a higher level of detail or using pre-aggregated fields. This can significantly reduce the number of calculations and improve performance.

**13.4 Visualization Design for Performance**

Designing visualizations that are optimized for performance is essential. Consider the following techniques:

Simplify Complex Visualizations: Simplify complex visualizations by reducing the number of marks, axes, or data points displayed. Use filtering, aggregation, or data reduction techniques to simplify the visual representation.

Limit Displayed Data: Limit the amount of data displayed in your visualizations by applying appropriate filters or using parameter controls. This helps reduce the rendering time and improves interactivity.

Use Aggregated Extracts: When working with large datasets, consider using aggregated extracts to speed up rendering and interactivity. Aggregated extracts contain pre-computed values that can be displayed more quickly.

Optimize Map Visualizations: If you're using map visualizations, simplify the level of detail and reduce the number of data points displayed. Consider using aggregation or data densification techniques to optimize map performance.

## 13.5 Tableau Server Configuration

To optimize Tableau Server performance and scalability, consider the following configuration techniques:

Hardware Resources: Ensure that Tableau Server is running on hardware that meets the recommended specifications. Allocate sufficient CPU, memory, and disk space to handle the expected workload.

Concurrent User Limits: Set appropriate limits on the number of concurrent users allowed on Tableau Server. Adjust these limits based on the server's capacity and performance requirements.

Caching and Extract Refresh: Utilize caching and extract refresh settings to improve performance. Cache frequently accessed views and schedule extract refreshes during low-usage periods to minimize impact on server performance.

Load Balancing: Implement load balancing across multiple Tableau Server instances to distribute the user load and improve overall performance. This ensures that the workload is evenly distributed and prevents any single server from becoming a bottleneck.

### 13.6 Testing and Monitoring

Regular testing and monitoring are essential to identify performance issues and optimize Tableau workbooks. Consider the following steps:

Load Testing: Perform load testing to simulate heavy user loads and identify any performance bottlenecks. This helps you understand the system's capacity and identify areas for optimization.

Workbook Performance Monitoring: Monitor workbook performance using Tableau Server's monitoring tools or third-party monitoring solutions. Track response times, query durations, and resource utilization to identify areas for improvement.

Query Performance Optimization: Analyze slow-performing queries and optimize them by adding appropriate indexes, rewriting queries, or adjusting data source configurations.

User Feedback: Gather feedback from users regarding performance and usability. Identify common pain points and areas of improvement based on user experiences and observations.

By implementing these performance optimization and scalability techniques in Tableau, you can enhance the speed, efficiency, and scalability of your workbooks, enabling you to work with larger datasets and deliver a seamless user experience.

Congratulations! In this chapter, you learned about performance optimization and scalability in Tableau. You explored techniques for data source optimization, calculation efficiency, visualization design, Tableau Server configuration, and testing and monitoring. By incorporating these practices, you can optimize your Tableau workbooks for improved performance and scalability. In the final chapter, we will discuss data security and best practices for ensuring the confidentiality and integrity of your data in Tableau.

# Chapter 14: Data Security and Best Practices in Tableau

## 14.1 Introduction to Data Security in Tableau

Data security is of utmost importance when working with sensitive or confidential data in Tableau. In this chapter, we will explore best practices and techniques to ensure the confidentiality, integrity, and availability of your data. Let's delve into data security and best practices in Tableau:

Access Control: Implement proper access control measures to restrict data access based on user roles and permissions.

Data Encryption: Protect your data by implementing encryption techniques to secure data at rest and in transit.

Data Masking: Apply data masking techniques to conceal sensitive information and ensure privacy.

Tableau Server Security: Configure Tableau Server with appropriate security settings to protect data and control user access.

**14.2 Access Control**

To ensure proper access control in Tableau, consider the following best practices:

User Authentication: Implement strong user authentication mechanisms, such as LDAP, Active Directory, or SAML, to verify user identities and prevent unauthorized access.

User Roles and Permissions: Define user roles and assign appropriate permissions based on job responsibilities and data access requirements. Restrict access to sensitive data and limit administrative privileges to authorized personnel.

Row-Level Security: Utilize row-level security to control access to specific rows of data based on user attributes or membership in specific groups. This ensures that users can only see the data relevant to their roles.

Two-Factor Authentication: Enable two-factor authentication for Tableau Server to provide an extra layer of security and prevent unauthorized access.

## 14.3 Data Encryption

Implementing data encryption techniques helps protect data from unauthorized access. Consider the following best practices:

Data at Rest Encryption: Enable data-at-rest encryption for Tableau Server by encrypting the underlying data files. This protects data stored on disk from unauthorized access.

SSL/TLS Encryption: Implement SSL/TLS encryption to secure data transmitted between Tableau Server and clients. Enable SSL/TLS protocols and configure trusted certificates to ensure secure communication.

Database Encryption: If your data resides in external databases, enable database-level encryption to protect data at the source. Consult your database vendor's documentation for encryption options and best practices.

Data Source Credentials: Securely manage data source credentials by utilizing password encryption or integrated authentication mechanisms. Avoid storing plain-text passwords and ensure secure handling of authentication information.

## 14.4 Data Masking

Data masking techniques help protect sensitive information while maintaining the usability of the data. Consider the following best practices:

Dynamic Data Masking: Use dynamic data masking techniques to conceal sensitive information in Tableau visualizations. Dynamically mask data based on user roles or permissions, ensuring that sensitive information is hidden from unauthorized users.

Anonymization: Anonymize sensitive data by replacing identifiable information with pseudonyms or generalized values. This technique protects privacy while preserving data integrity for analysis purposes.

Aggregation and Sampling: When working with sensitive data, consider aggregating or sampling data to reduce the risk of exposing personally identifiable information. This allows for analysis while minimizing the risk of data breaches.

Secure Data Publishing: When publishing data extracts or workbooks, ensure that sensitive information is not inadvertently exposed. Remove or mask confidential data fields, and review the published content before making it available to users.

**14.5 Tableau Server Security**

Configure Tableau Server with appropriate security settings to protect data and control user access. Consider the following best practices:

Server Hardening: Implement server hardening measures by following Tableau's security recommendations. Disable unnecessary services, apply security patches promptly, and restrict remote access to the server.

Firewall Configuration: Configure firewalls to allow only necessary network traffic to reach Tableau Server. Limit access to specific IP addresses or subnets to minimize the attack surface.

Backup and Recovery: Regularly back up Tableau Server configurations, data sources, and workbooks. Develop a comprehensive backup and recovery plan to ensure business continuity in the event of data loss or server failure.

Auditing and Monitoring: Enable auditing and monitoring features in Tableau Server to track user activities, detect anomalies, and investigate potential security breaches. Regularly review audit logs to identify any suspicious or unauthorized activities.

## 14.6 User Training and Awareness

Educating users about data security best practices is essential to ensure compliance and mitigate risks. Consider the following steps:

Security Awareness Training: Provide comprehensive security awareness training to all Tableau users. Train them on data handling best practices, password security, and the importance of following security policies.

Data Governance Policies: Establish data governance policies that outline the proper handling, storage, and sharing of data within Tableau. Communicate these policies to all users and ensure their compliance.

Incident Response Plan: Develop an incident response plan that outlines the steps to be taken in the event of a security incident or data breach. Train users on their roles and responsibilities within the plan.

Regular Security Updates: Keep users informed about the latest security updates, vulnerabilities, and best practices related to Tableau. Provide regular updates and reminders to reinforce security awareness.

By implementing these data security best practices in Tableau, you can ensure the confidentiality, integrity, and availability of your data. Protecting sensitive information and establishing a secure environment will help you comply with data privacy regulations and safeguard your organization's valuable assets.

Congratulations! In this chapter, you learned about data security and best practices in Tableau. You explored access control, data encryption, data masking, Tableau Server security, and user training and awareness. By following these practices, you can establish a secure and trustworthy environment for working with data in Tableau. With this knowledge, you are now equipped to harness the full potential of Tableau while maintaining the highest standards of data security.

# Chapter 15: Tableau Extensions: Enhancing Functionality and Customization

## 15.1 Introduction to Tableau Extensions

Tableau Extensions allow you to extend the functionality and customization capabilities of Tableau beyond its native features. In this chapter, we will explore the concept of Tableau Extensions and learn how to leverage them to enhance your Tableau experience. Let's delve into Tableau Extensions:

What are Tableau Extensions? Tableau Extensions are add-ons that integrate with Tableau to provide additional functionality, interactivity, and customization options.

Types of Tableau Extensions: There are various types of Tableau Extensions, including dashboard extensions, data connectors, web data connectors, and more. Each type serves a different purpose and offers unique capabilities.

Benefits of Using Tableau Extensions: Tableau Extensions offer benefits such as enhanced interactivity, advanced visualizations, external data integration, custom integrations, and improved user experiences.

## 15.2 Dashboard Extensions

Dashboard extensions allow you to incorporate external functionalities directly into your Tableau dashboards. Let's explore how to use dashboard extensions:

Extension Marketplace: Visit the Tableau Extension Marketplace to explore a wide range of available extensions. Browse through the extensions and identify the ones that suit your needs.

Installation: Install the desired extension by following the instructions provided in the marketplace. Extensions can be installed at the user or server level.

Adding Extensions to Dashboards: Once installed, you can add extensions to your dashboards. Open a dashboard in Tableau, navigate to the Extensions pane, and drag and drop the desired extension onto the canvas.

Configuration: Configure the extension by providing necessary information or parameters, such as API keys, data sources, or settings specific to the extension functionality.

Interaction: Interact with the extension by utilizing its features and options. Extensions can offer interactivity, data manipulation, external data retrieval, or other functionalities based on their purpose.

## 15.3 Data Connectors

Data connectors enable you to connect Tableau to external data sources that are not natively supported. Let's explore how to use data connectors:

Connector Types: Tableau supports various data connectors, including custom SQL connectors, ODBC connectors, REST API connectors, and more. Choose the appropriate connector based on your data source requirements.

Connector Installation: Install the required data connector software or libraries on your machine. Follow the instructions provided by the connector's documentation or the Tableau community.

Connection Setup: In Tableau, navigate to the Connect pane and select the appropriate connector type. Enter the necessary connection details, such as server address, port, authentication credentials, or API endpoints.

Data Retrieval: Once the connection is established, you can retrieve data from the external data source. Use the connector's options or query editor to specify the data to be retrieved and any required transformations.

Data Integration: Integrate the external data with your Tableau workbook by joining or blending it with existing data sources. Perform data cleansing, filtering, or aggregation as needed to create meaningful visualizations.

**15.4 Web Data Connectors**

Web data connectors enable you to retrieve data from web-based APIs or web scraping. Let's explore how to use web data connectors:

Web Data Connector Gallery: Visit the Tableau Web Data Connector Gallery or explore third-party resources to find pre-built web data connectors. Look for connectors that are compatible with your data sources or APIs.

Connector Installation: Install the web data connector by following the instructions provided in the connector documentation. Most web data connectors are JavaScript-based and require hosting on a web server.

Connection Setup: In Tableau, navigate to the Web Data Connector option in the Connect pane. Enter the URL or address of the web data connector you installed.

Authentication and Parameters: If required, provide authentication credentials or parameters specific to the web data source. This may include API keys, access tokens, or other necessary information.

Data Retrieval and Integration: Once the web data connector is connected, you can retrieve data from the web source. Use the connector's interface to specify the data to be retrieved, apply any necessary filters or transformations, and integrate the data with your Tableau workbook.

**15.5 Custom Visualization Extensions**

Custom visualization extensions allow you to create and integrate your own custom visualizations into Tableau. Let's explore how to create custom visualization extensions:

Development Environment Setup: Set up a development environment with the necessary tools and libraries for building Tableau custom visualization extensions. Tableau provides developer resources, SDKs, and samples to help you get started.

Extension Framework: Understand the Tableau extension framework, including the required files, code structure, and supported technologies. Follow the documentation and guidelines provided by Tableau for creating custom visualizations.

Visualization Design and Development: Design and develop your custom visualization using HTML, CSS, JavaScript, or other web technologies. Utilize the Tableau APIs and libraries to interact with Tableau data and features.

Packaging and Installation: Package your custom visualization as a Tableau extension file (.trex) and follow the installation instructions provided by Tableau. Distribute the extension file to other Tableau users as needed.

Integration and Usage: Once installed, your custom visualization extension can be added to Tableau dashboards. Drag and drop the extension onto the canvas, configure any required settings, and utilize the custom visualization in your data analysis and presentation.

## 15.6 Extension Considerations

When using Tableau extensions, consider the following points:

Compatibility: Ensure that the extension you choose is compatible with your Tableau version and meets your specific requirements.

Security and Trust: Evaluate the trustworthiness and security of third-party extensions before installation. Review user reviews, ratings, and recommendations to assess their reliability.

Extension Updates: Keep track of extension updates and new releases. Stay informed about bug fixes, feature enhancements, and security patches.

Community Support: Engage with the Tableau community, forums, and user groups to seek advice, share experiences, and troubleshoot any issues related to Tableau extensions.

By utilizing Tableau Extensions, you can enhance the functionality, interactivity, and customization of your Tableau workbooks. Whether it's incorporating external features, integrating data from non-native sources, or creating your own visualizations, extensions empower you to take your Tableau experience to the next level.

Congratulations! In this chapter, you learned about Tableau Extensions. You explored dashboard extensions, data connectors, web data connectors, and custom visualization extensions. By leveraging these extension capabilities, you can extend Tableau's functionality and customize your data analysis and visualization workflows. With this knowledge, you are now equipped to explore and utilize the vast world of Tableau Extensions to unlock new possibilities and insights.

# Chapter 16: Collaboration and Sharing in Tableau

## 16.1 Introduction to Collaboration and Sharing in Tableau

Collaboration and sharing are integral aspects of working with Tableau. In this chapter, we will explore the various features and techniques available in Tableau for collaborating with others, sharing your insights, and fostering a collaborative data culture. Let's dive into collaboration and sharing in Tableau:

Collaboration Benefits: Collaboration enables multiple users to work together, share knowledge, and contribute to data analysis and decision-making processes. It fosters teamwork, improves efficiency, and facilitates collective insights.

Sharing Options: Tableau offers several sharing options, including publishing to Tableau Server, Tableau Public, embedding in websites, and exporting to different file formats. Each option caters to different needs and levels of accessibility.

Collaboration Features: Tableau provides built-in collaboration features such as comments, subscriptions, and data-driven alerts. These features facilitate communication, automate updates, and ensure timely access to data insights.

## 16.2 Publishing to Tableau Server

Tableau Server enables you to publish workbooks and data sources, providing a centralized platform for collaboration and sharing. Let's explore how to publish to Tableau Server:

Prepare your Workbook: Ensure that your workbook is complete, validated, and ready for sharing. Review your visualizations, data connections, and calculations to ensure accuracy.

Publish to Tableau Server: In Tableau Desktop, go to the Server menu and select "Publish Workbook." Enter the necessary connection details, such as the server URL, authentication credentials, and the project where you want to publish the workbook.

Configure Permissions: Set permissions and access levels for the published workbook. Define who can view, edit, or interact with the workbook based on user roles and project requirements.

Data Source Publishing: If your workbook relies on external data sources, consider publishing those data sources separately. This ensures data consistency and allows other users to connect to the published data sources.

Collaborate and Share: Once published, users with appropriate permissions can access and interact with the workbook on Tableau Server. They can view, filter, and interact with visualizations, add comments, and collaborate with other users.

**16.3 Publishing to Tableau Public**

Tableau Public is a free platform for sharing interactive visualizations with a wider audience. Let's explore how to publish to Tableau Public:

Prepare your Workbook: Ensure that your workbook is optimized for public sharing. Review visualizations, data sources, and sensitive information that should be removed or anonymized.

Publish to Tableau Public: In Tableau Desktop, go to the Server menu and select "Tableau Public." Sign in to your

Tableau Public account or create a new one if necessary. Provide a title, description, and tags for your visualization.

Choose Visibility Options: Decide whether you want to make your visualization publicly visible or unlisted (accessible only via the direct URL). Set the visibility option that aligns with your sharing requirements.

Publish and Share: Click "Publish" to upload your workbook to Tableau Public. Once published, your visualization will be available on the Tableau Public website, and you can share the URL with others.

Embedding in Websites: Tableau Public allows you to embed your visualizations in websites, blogs, or social media platforms. Use the embed code provided by Tableau Public to integrate your visualization seamlessly.

**16.4 Exporting and Sharing as File Formats**

Tableau provides options to export your workbooks and visualizations into different file formats for sharing and collaboration. Let's explore exporting and sharing as file formats:

Export to PDF: To export your workbook as a PDF, go to the File menu and select "Download as PDF." Choose the desired layout options and click "Download" to save the PDF file locally.

Export to Image Formats: Tableau allows you to export visualizations as image files, such as PNG, JPEG, or SVG. Right-click on a visualization, go to "Export" or "Download," and select the desired image format.

Export as PowerPoint: To export your workbook as a PowerPoint presentation, go to the File menu and select "Export as PowerPoint." This option converts your workbook into a series of slides.

Share Exported Files: Once exported, you can share the PDF, images, or PowerPoint files with others via email, file sharing platforms, or collaboration tools. Ensure that the recipients have the necessary software to open and view the exported files.

## 16.5 Collaboration Features in Tableau

Tableau provides built-in collaboration features that facilitate communication, automate updates, and ensure timely access to data insights. Let's explore these collaboration features:

Comments: Add comments to worksheets or dashboards to provide feedback, ask questions, or initiate discussions. Users can reply to comments, fostering collaboration and knowledge sharing.

Subscriptions: Set up subscriptions to receive regular updates on specific views or dashboards. Subscriptions can be customized to deliver updates via email or Tableau Server notifications.

Data-Driven Alerts: Create data-driven alerts to receive notifications when specific data conditions are met. Alerts can be based on thresholds, changes in data values, or other criteria that require attention.

Mobile Collaboration: Tableau Mobile enables collaboration on the go. Users can access and interact with visualizations, view comments, and receive updates on their mobile devices.

### 16.6 Tableau Community and Online Collaboration

Engaging with the Tableau community and online collaboration platforms can expand your knowledge, foster collaboration, and provide opportunities for learning and sharing. Consider the following:

Tableau Community: Join the Tableau Community forums to connect with other Tableau users, ask questions, share knowledge, and seek advice. Participate in discussions and explore user-generated resources and tips.

Social Media Groups: Explore Tableau-related groups and communities on platforms like LinkedIn, Twitter, and Facebook. Connect with like-minded individuals, follow Tableau experts, and stay updated on the latest trends and resources.

Online Collaboration Platforms: Utilize collaboration platforms like Slack, Microsoft Teams, or Google Workspace to create dedicated Tableau channels or workspaces. Collaborate with colleagues, share insights, and exchange ideas in a centralized and organized environment.

User Groups and Events: Attend Tableau user groups and community events, either in-person or virtually. These gatherings provide opportunities to network, learn from experts, and collaborate with fellow Tableau enthusiasts.

By leveraging the collaboration and sharing features in Tableau, you can foster a collaborative data culture, share insights effectively, and engage with a wider community. Whether it's publishing to Tableau Server, sharing on Tableau Public, or collaborating through comments and subscriptions, Tableau empowers you to connect, communicate, and share your data-driven insights with others.

Congratulations! In this chapter, you learned about collaboration and sharing in Tableau. You explored publishing to Tableau Server, sharing on Tableau Public, exporting as file formats, collaboration features, and online collaboration platforms. With these collaboration techniques and tools, you can effectively collaborate with others, share your insights, and contribute to a data-driven and collaborative environment.

# Chapter 17: Advanced Analytics in Tableau: Going Beyond Visualization

## 17.1 Introduction to Advanced Analytics in Tableau

Tableau is not just a visualization tool; it also offers a wide range of advanced analytics capabilities. In this chapter, we will explore the advanced analytics features in Tableau that go beyond visualization, allowing you to uncover deeper insights and make data-driven decisions. Let's dive into advanced analytics in Tableau:

Why Advanced Analytics? Advanced analytics techniques enable you to analyze complex data, detect patterns, make predictions, and uncover hidden insights that go beyond traditional visualizations.

Tableau's Advanced Analytics Capabilities: Tableau provides a rich set of advanced analytics features, including statistical functions, forecasting, clustering, regression, and integration with machine learning models.

Use Cases: Advanced analytics in Tableau can be applied to a wide range of use cases, such as sales forecasting, customer segmentation, anomaly detection, sentiment analysis, and more.

**17.2 Statistical Functions and Calculations**

Tableau offers a variety of statistical functions and calculations that allow you to perform advanced analytics tasks. Let's explore some of these functions:

Aggregations: Tableau provides a range of built-in aggregations, including sum, average, minimum, maximum, standard deviation, and percentiles. These functions help you summarize and analyze your data.

Statistical Tests: Tableau supports statistical tests such as t-tests, chi-square tests, correlation analysis, and regression analysis. These tests enable you to analyze relationships, test hypotheses, and identify significant patterns in your data.

Trend Lines and Reference Lines: Tableau allows you to add trend lines and reference lines to your visualizations. Trend lines can help you identify and analyze trends over time, while reference lines provide benchmarks for comparison.

Table Calculations: Tableau's table calculations allow you to perform calculations across multiple dimensions and measure values. You can calculate moving averages, percent of total, rank, and more, enabling deeper analysis and comparison.

## 17.3 Forecasting and Time Series Analysis

Tableau provides powerful forecasting capabilities that allow you to analyze and predict future trends based on historical data. Let's explore how to leverage forecasting in Tableau:

Adding a Forecast: In Tableau, you can add a forecast to a visualization with just a few clicks. Select the desired visualization, go to the Analytics pane, and choose "Forecast." Tableau will automatically generate a forecast based on your data.

Forecast Options: Tableau offers various options for customizing the forecast, such as selecting the forecast length, confidence intervals, and smoothing options. Adjust these settings based on your data and forecasting requirements.

Analyzing Forecast Results: Once the forecast is added, Tableau visualizes the forecasted values alongside the historical data. Analyze the forecasted trends, compare them with the actual data, and gain insights into future patterns and potential outcomes.

Time Series Analysis: Tableau provides additional features for time series analysis, such as seasonality detection, decomposition, and period-over-period comparisons. Utilize these capabilities to gain a deeper understanding of your time-based data.

**17.4 Clustering and Segmentation**

Clustering and segmentation techniques in Tableau enable you to group similar data points together based on their characteristics. This helps in understanding patterns, identifying customer segments, and making targeted decisions. Let's explore clustering and segmentation in Tableau:

Creating Clusters: In Tableau, you can perform clustering analysis by utilizing built-in clustering models or by connecting to external clustering algorithms. Configure the settings, such as the number of clusters and clustering method, to create meaningful clusters.

Cluster Analysis: Once clusters are created, Tableau visualizes the clusters using different colors or shapes, allowing you to identify distinct groups within your data. Analyze the characteristics of each cluster and explore the insights they provide.

Customer Segmentation: Apply clustering techniques to segment your customer base based on various attributes, such as demographics, purchasing behavior, or preferences. Use these segments to personalize marketing strategies, optimize customer experiences, and drive business growth.

Cohort Analysis: Tableau supports cohort analysis, which allows you to track and compare the behavior of specific groups over time. Analyze cohort patterns and identify trends or anomalies that can help you optimize marketing campaigns, product launches, or customer retention strategies.

## 17.5 Integration with Machine Learning Models

Tableau offers integration with external machine learning models, allowing you to leverage the power of advanced machine learning algorithms within the Tableau environment. Let's explore how to integrate machine learning models in Tableau:

Model Training and Export: Train a machine learning model using your preferred programming language or machine learning platform. Export the trained model in a format compatible with Tableau, such as PMML (Predictive Model Markup Language) or ONNX (Open Neural Network Exchange).

Integration with Tableau: In Tableau, connect to the exported machine learning model using the "R" or "Python" integration. Write code to load the model and make predictions on Tableau data.

Embedding Predictions: Embed the machine learning predictions into your Tableau visualization by creating calculated fields or using table calculations. Visualize and analyze the model predictions alongside other data points in your dashboard.

Real-Time Scoring: For real-time predictions, integrate your machine learning model with Tableau using APIs or web services. This allows you to make predictions on new data as it arrives, enabling up-to-date insights and decision-making.

## 17.6 Custom Analytical Functions and Extensions

Tableau provides options to create custom analytical functions and extensions, allowing you to extend the analytics capabilities beyond the built-in features. Let's explore how to create custom analytical functions and extensions:

Tableau Calculation Language: Tableau's calculation language, including formulas and functions, provides flexibility to create custom calculations based on your specific analytical requirements. Utilize calculated fields and table calculations to perform custom analytics.

Tableau Extensions API: Leverage the Tableau Extensions API to create custom analytics extensions. Develop extensions using web technologies like HTML, CSS, and JavaScript, and integrate them seamlessly within Tableau to perform advanced analytics tasks.

Community Extensions: Explore the Tableau Extension Marketplace and Tableau community resources to find pre-built extensions created by other users. These extensions can provide additional advanced analytics functionalities that can be easily integrated into your Tableau workflows.

Third-Party Integrations: Tableau allows integration with external analytics platforms and tools. Leverage third-party analytics solutions by connecting them to Tableau, enabling you to leverage their advanced analytics capabilities within the Tableau environment.

By utilizing advanced analytics featuresin Tableau, you can go beyond basic visualization and uncover deeper insights in your data. Whether it's performing statistical analysis, forecasting future trends, clustering data points, integrating machine learning models, or creating custom analytical functions, Tableau provides a powerful platform for advanced analytics.

Congratulations! In this chapter, you learned about advanced analytics in Tableau. You explored statistical functions and calculations, forecasting and time series analysis, clustering and segmentation, integration with machine learning models, and the creation of custom analytical functions and extensions. With these advanced analytics capabilities, you can unlock deeper insights, make data-driven decisions, and gain a competitive edge in your data analysis journey with Tableau.

# Chapter 18: Tableau Server Administration: Managing and Optimizing Tableau Server

## 18.1 Introduction to Tableau Server Administration

Tableau Server is a robust platform that allows organizations to share, collaborate, and distribute Tableau content securely. In this chapter, we will explore Tableau Server administration, covering essential tasks and best practices for managing and optimizing Tableau Server. Let's dive into Tableau Server administration:

Importance of Server Administration: Effective Tableau Server administration ensures the stability, performance, security, and scalability of the Tableau environment. It enables smooth user experiences and maximizes the value of Tableau for the organization.

Server Administrator Roles: Tableau Server provides various administrator roles, such as the Server Administrator, Site Administrator, and Content Administrator. Each role has different responsibilities and permissions within the server environment.

Server Configuration and Monitoring: Server administration involves configuring server settings, monitoring server performance, managing licenses, and implementing security measures.

## 18.2 Server Installation and Configuration

Setting up and configuring Tableau Server correctly is crucial for a smooth deployment. Let's explore the installation and configuration process:

System Requirements: Review the Tableau Server system requirements to ensure that your server environment meets the necessary hardware, software, and network specifications.

Installation: Follow the Tableau Server installation guide provided by Tableau to install Tableau Server on your designated server machine. Choose the appropriate installation option (single node or multi-node) based on your deployment requirements.

Initial Configuration: After installation, configure the essential settings such as server name, administrator credentials, server port, and authentication method. Set up the server to match your organization's security policies and requirements.

License Activation: Activate your Tableau Server license to enable all the features and functionality provided by Tableau. Follow the instructions provided by Tableau to activate your license and ensure proper licensing compliance.

SSL/TLS Configuration: Implement SSL/TLS encryption to secure communication between Tableau clients and Tableau Server. Configure SSL/TLS certificates and protocols to establish secure connections and protect data in transit.

## 18.3 User and Group Management

Managing user access, roles, and permissions is a critical aspect of Tableau Server administration. Let's explore user and group management:

User Authentication: Integrate Tableau Server with your organization's existing authentication systems, such as Active Directory or SAML, to simplify user management and ensure a single sign-on experience.

User Roles and Permissions: Define user roles and assign appropriate permissions based on job responsibilities and data access requirements. Restrict access to sensitive data and limit administrative privileges to authorized personnel.

Group Management: Create user groups to efficiently manage permissions and access control. Assign users to appropriate groups based on their roles and responsibilities, simplifying permission management and user administration.

User Onboarding and Offboarding: Establish processes for user onboarding and offboarding. Ensure that new users are granted the necessary access and permissions, and remove access promptly when users leave the organization.

## 18.4 Content Management

Managing content on Tableau Server involves organizing, publishing, and maintaining workbooks, data sources, and dashboards. Let's explore content management:

Project Structure: Create a logical project structure that reflects your organization's hierarchy, teams, or departments. Organize content into projects to facilitate easy navigation and content discovery.

Workbook and Dashboard Publishing: Publish workbooks and dashboards to Tableau Server, ensuring that they are accessible to the intended users and groups. Consider permissions, data source dependencies, and best practices for efficient content publishing.

Version Control: Implement version control for workbooks and data sources to track changes, manage collaboration, and revert to previous versions if needed. Utilize version control systems or third-party tools to facilitate versioning and collaboration.

Content Refresh and Scheduling: Schedule automatic refreshes for data sources and extract-based workbooks to ensure up-to-date information for users. Set refresh intervals based on data freshness requirements and resource availability.

## 18.5 Performance Optimization

Optimizing Tableau Server performance ensures fast response times and efficient resource utilization. Let's explore performance optimization techniques:

Resource Monitoring: Regularly monitor server resource usage, such as CPU, memory, and disk space, to identify performance bottlenecks and plan for scalability. Utilize Tableau's built-in monitoring tools or third-party monitoring solutions for comprehensive monitoring.

Performance Tuning: Fine-tune Tableau Server settings to optimize performance. Adjust cache settings, query timeouts, and concurrent user limits based on server capacity, workload, and user requirements.

Extract Optimization: Optimize data extracts for faster query performance. Consider data extract filters, aggregation, and indexing techniques to reduce query response times and improve dashboard interactivity.

High Availability and Load Balancing: Implement high availability and load balancing configurations to ensure server uptime and distribute user traffic across multiple nodes. Configure load balancers and failover mechanisms for seamless user experiences.

### 18.6 Security and Governance

Maintaining the security and governance of Tableau Server is essential to protect sensitive data and comply with data privacy regulations. Let's explore security and governance practices:

Data Security: Implement access controls, encryption techniques, and data masking to protect sensitive information stored in Tableau Server. Ensure compliance with industry-specific security standards and regulations.

Authentication and Authorization: Configure strong authentication methods and granular authorization settings to ensure that users have appropriate access levels. Utilize single sign-on (SSO) solutions for seamless authentication across Tableau and other enterprise systems.

Data Governance: Establish data governance policies and processes to ensure data quality, consistency, and integrity. Implement data lineage tracking, metadata management, and data cataloging practices to enhance data governance.

Auditing and Compliance: Enable auditing features in Tableau Server to track user activities, data access, and changes to content. Regularly review audit logs and conduct security assessments to identify and mitigate potential vulnerabilities.

**18.7 Backup and Disaster Recovery**

Implementing a backup and disaster recovery strategy is crucial to protect your Tableau Server environment and ensure business continuity. Let's explore backup and disaster recovery best practices:

Regular Backups: Schedule regular backups of Tableau Server data, including workbooks, data sources, configuration files, and the underlying database. Store backups in secure locations, separate from the production environment.

Disaster Recovery Plan: Develop a comprehensive disaster recovery plan that outlines the steps to be taken in the event of server failure, data loss, or other emergencies. Test the plan periodically to ensure its effectiveness.

Testing and Validation: Perform backup and disaster recovery tests to validate the integrity and recoverability of your backups. Regularly restore backups to test the restoration process and verify that the data is recoverable.

Documentation: Document the backup and disaster recovery procedures, including backup schedules, recovery steps, and contact information for key personnel. Keep the documentation up to date and easily accessible to the relevant stakeholders.

By effectively managing and optimizing Tableau Server, you can ensure a secure, performant, and scalable environment for sharing and collaborating on Tableau content. By following the best practices outlined in this chapter, you can maximize the value of Tableau Server and provide a seamless user experience for your organization.

Congratulations! In this chapter, you learned about Tableau Server administration. You explored server installation and configuration, user and group management, content management, performance optimization, security and governance, and backup and disaster recovery. With this knowledge, you are equipped to effectively manage and optimize Tableau Server, enabling your organization to leverage the full potential of Tableaufor collaboration, data sharing, and decision-making.

# Chapter 19: Tableau Mobile: Exploring Data on the Go

## 19.1 Introduction to Tableau Mobile

Tableau Mobile allows you to access and explore your Tableau content on mobile devices, providing a seamless experience for data analysis and decision-making on the go. In this chapter, we will explore Tableau Mobile and learn how to leverage its features to effectively work with Tableau on mobile devices. Let's dive into Tableau Mobile:

Mobile Data Analysis: Tableau Mobile enables you to view and interact with your Tableau dashboards, visualizations, and reports on smartphones and tablets. It empowers you to explore data, gain insights, and make informed decisions anytime, anywhere.

Native Mobile App: Tableau Mobile is available as a native app for iOS and Android devices. You can download the app from the respective app stores and log in using your Tableau Server or Tableau Online credentials.

Mobile-Friendly Interface: Tableau Mobile provides an intuitive and mobile-friendly interface that is optimized for touch interaction. It allows you to navigate through dashboards, filter data, and interact with visualizations using gestures and taps.

**19.2 Navigating Tableau Mobile**

Let's explore how to navigate Tableau Mobile and access your Tableau content:

Dashboard Navigation: Upon launching Tableau Mobile, you will see a list of available dashboards. Swipe left or right to browse through the dashboards. Tap on a dashboard to open it for further exploration.

Interacting with Dashboards: Once a dashboard is open, you can interact with the visualizations by tapping on them, zooming in or out, and using touch gestures to explore the data. Use pinch gestures to zoom in or out, swipe to scroll, and tap to interact with data points.

Filtering Data: Tableau Mobile allows you to apply filters to dashboards directly from your mobile device. Tap on a filter option to select or deselect values and see the updated visualizations in real-time.

Exploring Sheets and Reports: In addition to dashboards, Tableau Mobile enables you to access individual sheets and reports. Navigate to the "Sheets" or "Reports" tab to explore and interact with specific visualizations or reports.

## 19.3 Collaboration and Sharing in Tableau Mobile

Tableau Mobile facilitates collaboration and sharing of insights with other users. Let's explore the collaboration features available in Tableau Mobile:

Sharing Dashboards: Share dashboards with others using Tableau Mobile. Tap on the "Share" icon within a dashboard to send the dashboard link via email, messaging apps, or other sharing options available on your mobile device.

Commenting and Discussions: Engage in discussions and provide feedback on dashboards using the commenting feature. Add comments to specific visualizations or respond to existing comments, fostering collaboration and knowledge sharing.

Subscriptions and Alerts: Stay updated on your data by subscribing to dashboards or specific visualizations. Set up subscriptions to receive regular email notifications or push notifications on your mobile device when the data changes or meets specific criteria.

**19.4 Offline Access and Data Refresh**

Tableau Mobile offers offline access to your Tableau content, allowing you to view and explore dashboards even without an internet connection. Let's explore offline access and data refresh:

Syncing Dashboards for Offline Access: Prior to going offline, you can sync dashboards to your mobile device for offline access. Simply tap on the "Sync" button within a dashboard to download it to your device. Syncing ensures that you have the latest data available offline.

Offline Interactions: While offline, you can interact with the synced dashboards, apply filters, and explore the data. Note that any changes or interactions made offline will be reflected only on your device and won't be visible to other users until you reconnect to the internet.

Data Refresh: When you reconnect to the internet, Tableau Mobile automatically refreshes the synced dashboards to fetch the latest data from Tableau Server or Tableau Online.

This ensures that you have up-to-date information when working online.

**19.5 Security and Authentication**

Tableau Mobile prioritizes data security and provides authentication options to protect your Tableau content. Let's explore security and authentication features:

Authentication Methods: Tableau Mobile supports various authentication methods, including Tableau Server credentials, Single Sign-On (SSO) with SAML, and OAuth authentication. Choose the authentication method that aligns with your organization's security policies.

Mobile Device Management (MDM) Integration: If your organization utilizes Mobile Device Management solutions, you can integrate Tableau Mobile with your MDM platform to enforce security policies, configure device-specific settings, and ensure secure access to Tableau content.

Remote Wipe and Data Encryption: In the event of a lost or stolen device, Tableau Mobile provides the capability to remotely wipe the Tableau content from the device to protect sensitive data. Additionally, Tableau Mobile encrypts data in transit and at rest to ensure data security.

**19.6 Tableau Mobile Best Practices**

To optimize your Tableau Mobile experience, consider the following best practices:

Mobile-Optimized Dashboards: Design dashboards specifically for mobile consumption, considering the screen size, touch interaction, and performance. Use mobile layout options in Tableau Desktop to create responsive dashboards that adapt to different screen sizes.

Performance Considerations: Optimize your dashboards for mobile performance by limiting the number of visualizations, reducing complex calculations, and utilizing extracts for faster data retrieval. Consider the bandwidth and connectivity of mobile devices when designing dashboards.

Data Security and Permissions: Implement appropriate permissions and access controls for mobile users to ensure that they can only access the data they are authorized to see. Apply consistent security measures across both Tableau Desktop and Tableau Mobile.

Training and User Adoption: Provide training and resources to users on how to effectively use Tableau Mobile. Educate them on the features, navigation, and best practices for mobile data analysis. Encourage user adoption to maximize the benefits of Tableau Mobile within your organization.

By leveraging Tableau Mobile, you can access your Tableau content on mobile devices, explore data, collaborate with others, and make data-driven decisions on the go. Whether it's navigating dashboards, interacting with visualizations, or sharing insights, Tableau Mobile empowers you to stay connected with your data wherever you are.

Congratulations! In this chapter, you learned about Tableau Mobile. You explored how to navigate Tableau Mobile, interact with dashboards, collaborate and share insights, access content offline, ensure security and authentication, and implement best practices for an optimal mobile experience. With Tableau Mobile, you can unlock the power of Tableau on your mobile device and make data-driven decisions anytime, anywhere.

## Chapter 20: Tableau and Big Data Integration: Analyzing Large-Scale Data

### 20.1 Introduction to Tableau and Big Data Integration

Tableau's integration with big data technologies allows you to analyze and visualize large-scale datasets efficiently. In this chapter, we will explore how to integrate Tableau with big data sources, leverage data connectors, and optimize performance for analyzing big data in Tableau. Let's dive into Tableau and big data integration:

Importance of Big Data Integration: Big data brings immense opportunities for organizations to derive insights and make data-driven decisions. Integrating Tableau with big data technologies enables you to analyze and visualize vast volumes of data in a user-friendly and intuitive interface.

Big Data Connectors: Tableau provides connectors to various big data technologies such as Apache Hadoop, Amazon Redshift, Google BigQuery, Apache Spark, and more. These connectors enable seamless integration and direct connectivity to big data sources.

Performance Considerations: Analyzing big data in Tableau requires optimization to handle the scale and complexity of the data. We will explore performance considerations and techniques for efficient big data analysis in Tableau.

## 20.2 Connecting to Big Data Sources

Let's explore how to connect Tableau to big data sources and establish the necessary connections:

Tableau Data Connectors: Tableau offers built-in data connectors specifically designed for connecting to big data sources. These connectors allow you to establish a connection to the desired big data platform seamlessly.

Configuring Connection Details: When connecting to a big data source, provide the necessary connection details such as server address, port, authentication credentials, and database or schema information. These details may vary depending on the specific big data technology you are connecting to.

Importing Data: After establishing the connection, you can import data from big data sources into Tableau. Specify the data tables, files, or queries you want to import, and Tableau will retrieve the data and make it available for analysis.

Extracts vs. Live Connections: Tableau offers two options for working with big data sources: extracts and live connections. Extracts involve importing a subset or aggregated data into Tableau's proprietary data engine, while live connections allow you to query the data directly from the source. Choose the option that best suits your analysis requirements and performance considerations.

**20.3 Performance Optimization for Big Data Analysis**

Optimizing performance is crucial when working with big data in Tableau. Let's explore techniques to enhance performance for big data analysis:

Data Source Filters: Leverage data source filters to limit the amount of data retrieved from the big data source. Apply filters early in the analysis process to reduce the dataset size and improve query performance.

Aggregations and Summaries: Utilize aggregations and summary calculations to pre-aggregate the data before visualization. This minimizes the amount of data processed and improves the response time for queries and visualizations.

Extract Optimization: When working with big data, consider creating data extracts in Tableau to improve performance. Extracts allow you to subset, filter, and aggregate the data before analysis, resulting in faster query response times.

Data Source Joins: Optimize data source joins by using appropriate join techniques, such as utilizing indexes or performing join operations in the big data platform itself. Properly configuring joins reduces the data volume and improves query performance.

Parallel Processing: Leverage Tableau's parallel processing capabilities to speed up queries and calculations. Enable parallel processing for data blending, calculations, and other operations to take advantage of the underlying hardware resources.

**20.4 Leveraging Big Data Platforms and Technologies**

Integrating Tableau with big data platforms and technologies allows you to leverage their capabilities for efficient data analysis. Let's explore some popular big data platforms and technologies:

Apache Hadoop: Connect Tableau to Apache Hadoop, a distributed computing framework, to analyze data stored in Hadoop Distributed File System (HDFS) or Hadoop-compatible file systems. Leverage the power of Hadoop's scalability and data processing capabilities within Tableau.

Amazon Redshift: Connect Tableau to Amazon Redshift, a fully-managed data warehousing service, for fast and scalable analysis of large datasets. Utilize Redshift's columnar storage and parallel query execution to optimize performance.

Google BigQuery: Integrate Tableau with Google BigQuery, a serverless data warehouse, to analyze massive datasets with high performance and flexibility. Leverage BigQuery's serverless architecture and SQL-like querying capabilities within Tableau.

Apache Spark: Connect Tableau to Apache Spark, a fast and distributed data processing engine, to analyze big data stored in Spark clusters. Leverage Spark's in-memory processing capabilities and advanced analytics libraries within Tableau.

**20.5 Advanced Analytics on Big Data in Tableau**

Tableau provides advanced analytics capabilities that can be applied to big data analysis. Let's explore advanced analytics techniques for big data in Tableau:

Statistical Analysis: Utilize Tableau's statistical functions and calculations to perform statistical analysis on big data. Perform aggregations, correlations, regressions, and other statistical calculations to uncover patterns and relationships in your data.

Machine Learning Integration: Integrate Tableau with machine learning platforms or libraries to apply advanced machine learning algorithms to big data analysis. Leverage the power of machine learning models for predictive analytics, clustering, or anomaly detection.

Spatial Analysis: If your big data contains spatial or location-based information, Tableau's spatial analysis capabilities can help you visualize and analyze geospatial patterns. Perform spatial aggregations, create heat maps, or overlay data on maps to gain insights from spatial data.

Data Blending and Mashups: Combine big data with other datasets using Tableau's data blending and data integration capabilities. Blend data from multiple sources to gain a comprehensive view and perform cross-source analysis.

**20.6 Security Considerations for Big Data Integration**

When integrating Tableau with big data sources, it's essential to consider security measures to protect sensitive data. Let's explore security considerations for big data integration:

Access Controls: Implement access controls and permissions within Tableau to restrict user access to sensitive big data. Ensure that only authorized users can access, view, and analyze the data based on their roles and responsibilities.

Data Encryption: Enable encryption for data in transit and at rest when working with big data in Tableau. Utilize SSL/TLS encryption for secure communication between Tableau and the big data source, and leverage encryption mechanisms provided by the big data platform.

Authentication and Single Sign-On (SSO): Integrate Tableau with your organization's authentication systems and implement SSO to ensure secure access to big data sources.

Leverage existing authentication mechanisms to authenticate Tableau users and enforce access controls.

Auditing and Monitoring: Enable auditing features in Tableau to track user activities, data access, and changes made to big data sources. Regularly review audit logs and monitor data access to identify and mitigate potential security risks.

By integrating Tableau with big data sources, you can unlock the power of big data analytics and gain valuable insights from large-scale datasets. Whether it's connecting to big data sources, optimizing performance, leveraging big data platforms, or applying advanced analytics techniques, Tableau enables you to effectively analyze and visualize big data for informed decision-making.

Congratulations! In this chapter, you learned about Tableau and big data integration. You explored connecting to big data sources, optimizing performance, leveraging big data platforms and technologies, performing advanced analytics on big data, and considering security measures

# Chapter 21: Tableau and Geographic Data: Visualizing and Analyzing Spatial Information

## 21.1 Introduction to Tableau and Geographic Data

Tableau provides powerful capabilities for visualizing and analyzing geographic data, allowing you to gain insights from spatial information. In this chapter, we will explore how to work with geographic data in Tableau, leverage mapping features, and perform spatial analysis. Let's dive into Tableau and geographic data:

Importance of Geographic Data Analysis: Geographic data analysis enables you to understand patterns, relationships, and trends based on location. Tableau's mapping and spatial analysis features help you visualize and explore data in a geospatial context.

Types of Geographic Data: Geographic data can include various types such as points of interest, addresses, boundaries, latitude and longitude coordinates, and more. Tableau supports different geographic data formats, including shapefiles, KML files, spatial databases, and web services.

Mapping Capabilities: Tableau offers robust mapping capabilities, allowing you to create interactive maps, overlay data on maps, and perform spatial analysis. With Tableau, you can unlock the power of geographic visualization and make data-driven decisions based on location.

## 21.2 Working with Geographic Data in Tableau

Let's explore how to work with geographic data in Tableau, from connecting to spatial data sources to visualizing geographic information:

Connecting to Spatial Data Sources: Tableau provides various options for connecting to spatial data sources. You can connect directly to spatial databases such as PostgreSQL/PostGIS, Microsoft SQL Server, or utilize spatial file formats like shapefiles, KML, or GeoJSON.

Importing Geographic Data: Once connected to a spatial data source, import the geographic data into Tableau. Specify the geographic tables or files you want to import, and Tableau will retrieve the data and make it available for visualization and analysis.

Geocoding Addresses: If your data contains address information, Tableau can perform geocoding to convert addresses into latitude and longitude coordinates. Utilize Tableau's built-in geocoding functionality or connect to external geocoding services to enrich your data with spatial information.

Geographic Roles and Hierarchies: Tableau recognizes geographic fields and assigns them specific roles (e.g., country, state, city) to enable automatic geographic mapping. Verify and adjust geographic roles as needed to ensure accurate mapping of your data.

**21.3 Creating Geographic Visualizations in Tableau**

Let's explore how to create compelling geographic visualizations in Tableau to effectively communicate spatial insights:

Geographic Maps: Tableau allows you to create geographic maps by simply dragging and dropping geographic fields onto the view. Choose the appropriate map type (e.g., filled map, symbol map, choropleth map) to represent your data effectively.

Customizing Map Layers: Tableau provides options to customize map layers, including adding background maps, changing map styles, and adjusting map options such as zoom levels, pan, and rotation. Tailor the map appearance to suit your visualization requirements.

Data Overlay: Overlay additional data on maps to provide context and additional insights. Add data layers such as points of interest, boundaries, demographic information, or custom shapes to enrich your geographic visualizations.

Filtering and Highlighting: Utilize Tableau's filtering and highlighting capabilities to focus on specific geographic regions or data points of interest. Apply filters based on geographic fields, and highlight specific areas to emphasize patterns or outliers.

### 21.4 Spatial Analysis and Calculations

Tableau offers spatial analysis capabilities that allow you to perform calculations and derive insights from geographic data. Let's explore spatial analysis in Tableau:

Distance and Proximity Analysis: Calculate distances between points, find the nearest locations, or perform proximity analysis using Tableau's spatial calculations. Measure distances on maps, identify nearby points of interest, or create buffers around specific locations.

Spatial Joins: Combine geographic data with non-geographic data using spatial joins in Tableau. Perform spatial joins to associate geographic attributes with non-geographic data points, enabling comprehensive analysis and visualization.

Geospatial Aggregations: Tableau supports aggregating data based on geographic regions such as countries, states, or custom boundaries. Perform geospatial aggregations to understand patterns, calculate averages, or analyze distribution across geographic areas.

Spatial Interpolation: Utilize Tableau's interpolation capabilities to estimate values for unmeasured locations based on nearby observations. Apply spatial interpolation techniques to create smooth surfaces, heat maps, or contour maps.

## 21.5 Geographic Data Layers and Web Mapping Services

Tableau allows you to integrate additional data layers and leverage web mapping services to enhance your geographic visualizations. Let's explore data layers and web mapping services in Tableau:

Web Mapping Services: Connect Tableau to web mapping services such as Mapbox, ArcGIS Online, or OpenStreetMap to access additional map layers, basemaps, or spatial data services. Leverage these services to enrich your geographic visualizations with relevant context and information.

Custom Map Layers: Import custom map layers, such as shapefiles or GeoJSON files, to overlay additional geographic data on your Tableau maps. This enables you to incorporate external data sources or proprietary geospatial information into your visualizations.

WMS and WMTS Integration: Tableau supports integration with Web Map Services (WMS) and Web Map Tile Services (WMTS). Connect to WMS/WMTS sources to access pre-rendered map tiles or dynamically generated map images for precise and detailed map backgrounds.

Background Map Styling: Customize the appearance of background maps in Tableau by adjusting map styles, colors, labels, and map elements. Tailor the map styling to suit your visualization requirements and enhance the visual impact of your geographic visualizations.

**21.6 Dashboard Design Considerations for Geographic Visualizations**

When designing dashboards with geographic visualizations, consider the following best practices to effectively communicate spatial insights:

Map Size and Placement: Allocate sufficient space for maps on your dashboard to provide a clear view of geographic patterns and data points. Consider the overall layout and placement of maps to ensure they are easily interpretable and visually balanced.

Interactivity and Drill-Down: Enable interactivity in your geographic visualizations by leveraging Tableau's features such as tooltips, filters, and actions. Allow users to drill down into specific geographic regions or access additional details by interacting with the map.

Contextual Information: Provide contextual information and annotations on your dashboard to help users understand the significance of the geographic insights. Include captions, titles, legends, or annotations to provide additional context and clarify the implications of the data.

Responsive Design: Design your dashboards with responsive layouts to ensure optimal viewing experiences across different devices and screen sizes. Test the dashboard on various devices to ensure that the geographic visualizations adapt well to different screen resolutions.

By leveraging Tableau's capabilities for geographic data, you can gain valuable insights from spatial information, identify patterns, and make informed decisions based on location. Whether it's connecting to spatial data sources, visualizing geographic information, performing spatial analysis, or designing effective dashboards, Tableau empowers you to unlock the power of geographic data analysis.

Congratulations! In this chapter, you learned about Tableau and geographic data analysis. You explored connecting to spatial data sources, visualizing geographic data, performing spatial analysis, integrating data layers and web mapping services, and designing effective dashboards for geographic visualizations. With Tableau's geographic capabilities, you can effectively analyze and communicate insights from spatial information,making informed decisions and gaining a deeper understanding of your data in a geospatial context.

www.ingramcontent.com/pod-product-compliance
Lightning Source LLC
LaVergne TN
LVHW051344050326
832903LV00031B/3726